THIS IS A CARLTON BOOK

Text and Design copyright ©Carlton Books Limited 2001

This edition published by Carlton Books Limited 2001
20 Mortimer Street, London W1T 3JW

Printed and bound in Italy

ISBN 1 84222 461 1

Project editor: Luke Friend
Project art direction: Karen Kloot
Design: DW Design
Picture research: Debora Fioravanti
Production: Sarah Corteel

Contents

Introduction

It can be startling just to peer through the side window of a stationary Winston Cup car. Such stock car racers are capable of over 200 miles per hour, but are not much more than an engine, steel tubing, and sheet metal with a lone seat tucked in the middle, where a steering wheel hangs like an eternal full moon and beckons only the brave.

Since the birth of stock car racing in the post-war years, drivers have toiled with such rudimentary elements to demonstrate just who they were and what they could do. But none made as much from this potent, modern alchemy of passion and steel as Dale Earnhardt.

As long as these types of cars are raced on Saturday night short tracks and superspeedways, the legend of Earnhardt will live on. Long after that day when his uncompromising will to dominate NASCAR's premier Winston Cup series led to a fatal crash on the last lap of the Daytona 500, the name Earnhardt will evoke feelings of triumph and gritty majesty, especially among the hard-working fans who saw him as one of their own.

Born in the mill town of Kannapolis, N.C., the son of dirt track racer Ralph Earnhardt wasn't the first to drive a car fast enough to move from the working class to fame and to enough fortune to buy *"diamonds as big as horse chips,"* the way Dale put it when he first made the big time. He wasn't the first—or the last—whose fame carried the sport to new

that whatever tactics *"The Intimidator"* used against them, they were welcome to throw right back at him, the moral bedrock of the Earnhardt clan. Perhaps that was his most fearsome aspect of all: few were willing to fight that passionate fire on his terms.

Watching Earnhardt battle for the lead in a Winston Cup race—or even tenth place—was worth the price of admission. He brought an enduring value to his driving and life, a commitment that proved to be far more of an elixir than his impressive and long list of statistical accomplishments. He died standing on the gas, defending his territory, his way of life.

LEFT: Earnhardt always looked ahead, but never left behind his beginnings in a North Carolina mill town.

ABOVE LEFT: It was said Earnhardt could see the air at Talladega, where he had a record ten wins, including his final victory.

BELOW: Earnhardt was in seventh heaven when he won the race at Rockingham, N.C. and clinched his final Winston Cup in 1994.

heights of popularity. Others can be invoked as well when it comes to car control or a seat-of-the-pants feel for a thundering stock car.

Earnhardt excelled by living longer and closer to the edge of risk with more determination, bravery, and sheer love of the competition. He had more crashes at higher speeds, more amazing recoveries of errant cars, more breath-taking maneuvers to win races and more controversies when it came to running into other drivers. Ultimately, his style of driving changed the standard for what it took to win in the Winston Cup, stock car racing's most prestigious arena.

The fierce determination of Earnhardt sustained fear in the hearts of his competitors, who knew that Earnhardt believed the track was his until someone proved otherwise. They knew *"Ironhead"* would stubbornly withstand the angry words, the flailing fists, the boos and the penalties from NASCAR. They knew, also,

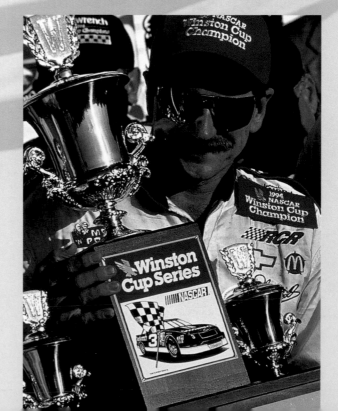

Blue Collar Dreams

Kannapolis, N.C., was a close-knit community in more ways than one when Ralph Dale Earnhardt was born on April 29, 1951.

A blue-collar town, the majority of people worked for Cannon Mills. The football team at Brown High School was the most popular sport, but quite a few worked the early shift at the mill from 7 a.m. until 3 p.m. and then in the afternoons and evenings worked on race cars, invariably neighborhood projects. The town also had an unruly edge on the Rowan County side, where beer was served curbside at numerous little drive-ins and fist fights broke out regularly.

The Earnhardt family lived near the corner of Coach and Sedan, where Ralph Earnhardt, a barnstorming race car driver, had a garage that would become the hothouse for Dale's race car driving dreams. He had two older sisters and two younger brothers, but it was Dale who had the constant hankering to become a racer, just like his father, who was the national

BELOW: Earnhardt and his younger brothers Randy (right) and Danny (middle) would all eventually go racing, but only Dale would follow his father's career as a driver.

champion in 1956 of NASCAR's Late Model Sportsman division.

"When he was in school, thinking about his dad going off racing would eat at him," said David Oliver, who would marry one of Dale's sisters and loan him his first race car. *"If his father had been off racing the night before, he couldn't wait to get home and go count the dents in the car."*

Ralph towed his car to dirt tracks all over the Carolinas and sometimes to Virginia and Georgia. A good driver could make a decent living by picking and choosing races that offered the best purses. The short races on bullrings in such places as Columbia, Savannah, Asheville, and Myrtle Beach were easy on tires and engines, if not fenders. Even at the outset of the 1960s, when the high-banked asphalt speedways sprang up in Daytona, Atlanta and nearby Charlotte, the weekly dirt tracks and their slam-bang action continued to draw hundreds of cars. Grandstands were full and the race action was furious, especially around Earnhardt's car, which scythed through fields like an eel on a binge. It carried number 8 on the side, a subtle form of intimidation since it was considered bad luck, one of the few numbers that looked the same whether the car was right side up or upside down.

The Late Model legend who let his driving do the talking would carry his sons to local tracks like Concord, N.C., where drivers from NASCAR's premier Grand National

series such as Junior Johnson would pick on young Dale, asking if he was going to be a race car driver like his daddy? When the races started, the boy would be all eyes, watching his father's every move from the family truck, so that when he finally sat in a race car nobody would have to give him any instruction.

Whatever odd jobs were available in his daddy's garage, Dale was there to take them on. He eventually would become an expert welder and could build engines from scratch like his virtuoso dad.

But words were scarce and sometimes scarcely grammatical from the quiet boy who would one day dub short track action in the Winston Cup as *"frammin' and bammin'."* When it came to instruction in school, the eagerness disappeared. Much against his father's wishes but like many other 16-year-olds in Kannapolis, Dale quit school in ninth grade at the earliest legal age. Only he vowed to never work in the mills. He was preparing to be a race car driver.

"When he was in school, thinking about his dad going off racing would eat at him"

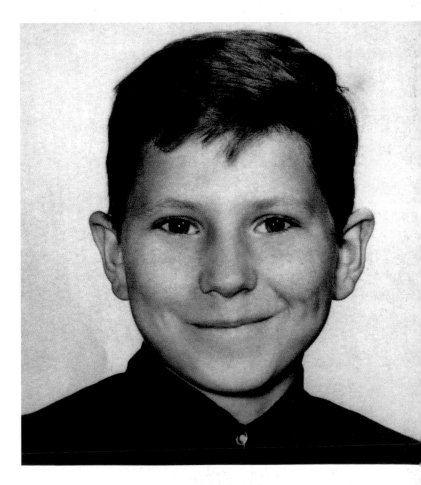

TOP: Ralph Earnhardt was a dirt track legend in the Carolinas, where a driver could make more money due to good purses and lower equipment costs than on the superspeedways built in the 60s.

BOTTOM LEFT: One year Ralph Earnhardt won 17 straight feature races at Hickory, N.C., which eventually hurt attendance and made the promoter so angry that toward the end of the streak he refused to present the trophy or let Earnhardt kiss the beauty queen in victory circle.

RIGHT: His fellow students invariably found young Dale Earnhardt to be a quiet boy; others considered him to be painfully shy.

Ragged Road To Riches

No driver ever worked harder under more difficult circumstances than Dale Earnhardt to make the long leap from stock car racing's minor leagues to the Winston Cup. Along the way, a rabble-rousing driving style tore up enough race cars to fill a junkyard.

Not long after quitting his job at Great Dane Trailer and ending his first marriage, Earnhardt began his racing career at age 20 in 1971. He drove a Ford loaned to him by brother-in-law David Oliver with an engine built by Ralph Earnhardt. Within two years, Earnhardt found other rides and won the championship at the Concord dirt track in 1972 and 1973.

Earnhardt *"knew everything about what made a race car go,"* said Oliver. *"He was always a hard worker and a hands-on guy."* Earnhardt thought he would eventually drive a second car for his legendary father. Those hopes ended in September of 1973, when Ralph Earnhardt died from a heart attack while working in his garage at the age of 45.

Though profoundly painful, that setback also allowed Earnhardt to look beyond the dirt tracks to the Winston Cup's increasing number of superspeedways. At the time, NASCAR was re-building its feeder system to the Winston Cup by emphasizing asphalt short tracks in its Sportsman division. H.A. *"Humpy"* Wheeler, the promoter at the nearby Charlotte Motor Speedway, was also emphasizing the need for new stars. *"If the Chicago Bears can have a star halfback at the age of 25, then NASCAR can have young drivers too,"* he said.

Eager to move up, Earnhardt bought an asphalt racer from veteran Harry Gant in 1974. He beat established stars Tommy Houston at Hickory Speedway and Bob Pressley at Metrolina Speedway that year and voiced his ambition to join the Winston Cup and *"to win the points championship."*

With support from Wheeler, Earnhardt found rides in both the Sportsman and Winston Cup races on Charlotte's high banks in 1975 with middling results. In 1976, he ventured to Atlanta's superspeedway, where

he flipped the Ford owned by Johnny Ray several times on the back straight, the first in a career of spectacular Winston Cup crashes. *"I wasn't hurt,"* he said, *"but I was crying because I was so sorry about tearing up Johnny Ray's car."*

Due to his tire and engine bills escalating on the asphalt short tracks, Earnhardt spent the next two years working odd jobs, fighting debt and the effects of a second divorce as well as a wreck in Asheville, N.C., that totaled his car. At times Earnhardt seemed wild in his sorrow over the death of his father, which only re-doubled his ambition to make it to the top. Fortunately, he got the advice he normally could have expected from his father from Wheeler, who persuaded him to go to work for his former father-in-law Robert Gee, a specialist in hanging body work on race car chassis who allowed Earnhardt to run his dirt track car.

Earnhardt's break finally arrived when a new Winston Cup team, where Earnhardt bought used parts, built an entry for him to run for the third time in Charlotte's annual Sportsman event in

Engine by

PREVIOUS PAGE: Earnhardt described himself as 'young and dumb' during the years he relentlessly chased an opportunity to join the Winston Cup. Once he arrived in the big leagues he not only looked bright, but right at home.

LEFT: His talent undeniable, the rides kept coming for Earnhardt, this one in 1978 in Huntsville, Ala.

October of 1978. California industrialist Rod Osterlund, who had moved his race operation to Charlotte the previous year, owned the team. In the Sportsman race, Earnhardt finished second to Bobby Allison. Next, Osterlund put him in a Winston Cup entry in Atlanta, where Earnhardt ran fourth behind Donnie Allison, Richard Petty and teammate Dave Marcis.

At the following Winston Cup season finale in Ontario, Calif., Marcis quit the Osterlund team after the race in protest against the firing of crew chief Dewey Livengood. Earnhardt, now 27, had driven a second entry once again for Osterlund and finished 11th. Afterward in the garage, the team owner showed Cale Yarborough, who had won his third championship that season, a list of driving prospects he was mulling over as a replacement for Marcis. *"Go with the young boy,"* advised Yarborough, referring to Earnhardt. Little did Yarborough realize that two years later at the exact same track, on board an Osterlund Racing Chevy, Earnhardt would beat him to the Winston Cup championship.

Rookie Season:
A Bruised Heart

When Dale Earnhardt entered the Winston Cup full time in 1979, he remained a rookie because he had not run more than five races in any one season. He thus joined one of the most talented crops of newcomers in NASCAR history. Terry Labonte, Harry Gant and road racer Al Holbert all vied against him for rookie of the year honors.

Earnhardt would eventually win seven championships and Labonte would win two Winston Cups. Gant, the oldest, was the runner-up in Labonte's first championship season in 1984 and would retire with 18 career victories. Although Holbert's bid to compete in NASCAR failed, he went on to win three more International Motor Sports Association Camel GT championships and three Le Mans 24-hour races.

But Earnhardt was the only one of them to win a race in the 1979 season, the first rookie to triumph in the Winston Cup in five years. He then fought his way back from an horrendous mid-season crash at Pocono, and the resulting concussion and two broken

collar bones. In his first race after returning, Earnhardt won the pole in Richmond, Va. and then went on to clinch the rookie title.

For the Osterlund Racing driver who became known as *"One Tough Customer"* under Wrangler Jeans sponsorship and who eventually was seen as a throwback to the backwoods, roughhewn days of NASCAR, it seemed fitting that Earnhardt won his first race at Bristol. *"The proper driving equipment,"* said that year's pole winner Buddy Baker of the steeply banked half-mile bowl in the Tennessee mountains, *"is a body cast from the waist up."*

Speeds and g-forces that wore a driver to the nub were not the only problems. Baker and Cale Yarborough tangled for the lead in Turn 4 on the 137th of 500 laps and crashed out. After qualifying ninth, Earnhardt eventually beat Bobby Allison by 2.7 seconds and won $19,800. *"I just wish my Dad had been there to see it,"* he said. In the ensuing decade, Earnhardt's dominance of the short tracks would be a crucial element in his championship success.

He would not have lived to win those

championships, or the rookie title, had he not survived the accident at Pocono, where a tire failure while leading and subsequent impact with the wall bruised his heart. Earnhardt's peculiar seat position might have saved his life. Riding low, his helmeted head hit the inside of the car hard enough to give him a concussion, but more catastrophic injuries could have occurred had his head gone outside the car's window. As it was, when Earnhardt recovered consciousness, the whites of his eyes had turned into a sea of blood red.

Earnhardt, who would miss four races while David Pearson substituted for him, recognized that out of sight was out of mind and perhaps out of a job. A press conference was arranged prior to the next race at Talladega. But it was conducted by telephone so reporters would not recognize the extent of his injuries. *"They said I bruised my heart,"* he joked. *"Heck, I've had a broken heart before. I'll get over it."*

The First Winston Cup

ABOVE: Earnhardt won all but three of his points races in the Winston Cup aboard a Chevy. One of the most famed versions was the No. 2 entry of Osterlund Racing that he drove to his first Winston Cup title in 1980. That was the last season for the monstrous 115-inch wheelbase cars. They weighed 3,700 pounds and steering required arms of steel.life.

Rod Osterlund liked to characterize the struggle between his team versus the established stars of the Winston Cup as *"college kids"* going up against the Super Bowl-winning *"Pittsburgh Steelers."* If so, sophomore driver Earnhardt and his crew took the teams of Cale Yarborough, Richard Petty and Darrell Waltrip to school during the 1980 season.

Compared to the powerhouse entries of Junior Johnson, Petty Enterprises and DiGard Racing, newcomer Osterlund's team was more akin to a high school squad.

Businessman Osterlund entered his third season with a second-year driver and only one win until the spring of 1980, when Earnhardt scored his first superspeedway victory in Atlanta after predicting, *"We can win the championship."*

Two months later, crew chief *"Suitcase"* Jake Elder packed his bags and was replaced by 20-year-old Doug Richert, barely past the rank of rookie mechanic. Just as a driver can carry an ill-handling chassis, it was Earnhardt who masked the team's mechanical weaknesses and held it together.

During the summer, Earnhardt's cocky prediction looked more credible when Petty had his own bad crash at Pocono. A bitterly unhappy Waltrip, meanwhile, was locked into a contract dispute with DiGard, leaving only three-time champion Yarborough and Johnson's team to contest the title. In August, Yarborough won two straight to pull within ten points of Earnhardt. The sophomore responded by winning his fourth and fifth races of the year at Martinsville, Va., and Charlotte in the fall. Yarborough countered with wins at Rockingham, N.C., and Atlanta.

Gunning to become the first second-year driver to win the title, Earnhardt brought a new dimension to a championship chase despite Yarborough's late-season charge. At Rockingham, even though he was a lap down, Earnhardt made aggressive moves on Yarborough, who angrily promised to give the upstart *"a lecture."*

In Atlanta, Earnhardt rode his Chevy side-by-side with Yarborough during the final three laps, despite having lost a lap midway in the race after getting caught in the pits by a caution. *"That's the worst piece of driving I've seen anybody do,"* fumed Yarborough. But Earnhardt again had given his team a psychological boost. *"Without that caution and lost lap, it would have been one hell of a finish,"* he said.

Next, in the finale at California's Ontario Motor Speedway, the youngster held on despite a wrong rear gear choice, another lap lost to bad pit strategy and a serious error on the final, woozy pit stop. After making up his lost lap, Earnhardt ran over his jack in the pits, then drove three laps with only two lug nuts on the right rear wheel before getting called back into the pits by NASCAR officials. If not for this standard penalty for running over his jack—and a chance to replace three lug nuts—Earnhardt might have literally driven a wheel off in the final 17 laps.

Earnhardt finished fifth, clinching the title by 19 points. Most thought him lucky, but Earnhardt's successful struggle to carry a third-year team to the title was the first of six more championships. For their part, Osterlund, team manager Roland Wlodyka, and Richert never participated in another Winston Cup title chase.

Broken Homes, Victory Lane

Where his father Ralph sustained a home for his wife and five children, Dale Earnhardt's pursuit of his racing dreams meant family hardships.

His first marriage at age 17 did not last long after son Kerry was born. Due to his mounting debts from racing, Earnhardt could offer little resistance when his first son was later adopted by his ex-wife's new husband. Earnhardt's second marriage to Brenda Gee was more promising, since her father owned and built race cars. Their daughter Kelly King was born in 1972 and Ralph Dale Jr. followed in 1974. But once again, the financial demands of racing scuttled the relationship. Earnhardt divorced a second time and again the destiny of his children was in doubt, which rankled him and often left him moody. It was not until after he won his first Winston Cup championship in 1980 that Earnhardt gained custody rights to Kelly and Dale Jr.

In 1982, the marriage to Teresa Houston proved to be a perfect fit. The beautiful niece of Busch Series regular Tommy Houston, Teresa not only accepted racing but also wanted to participate. She became instrumental in the establishment of Dale Earnhardt Inc. and in honing the rough edges to her husband's personality.

Their daughter Taylor Nicole was born in 1988. A devoted father, Earnhardt constantly counseled others in the Winston Cup garage to spend more time with their children and wives. *"He would meet his business obligations and then it was time for Taylor and Teresa,"* said Don Hawk, his former business manager.

Earnhardt guided each son's driving career. But just as his father before him,

Kerry and Dale Jr. had to demonstrate they really wanted to race. They started by alternating behind the wheel in a $200 Late Model Stock racer. But it was Dale Jr. who had his father's aggressive confidence and advanced to the Busch Series. *"June Bug"* won two championships driving for Dale Earnhardt Inc. before moving up to the Winston Cup in 2000 with a $10 million sponsorship from Budweiser in a Chevy numbered 8—just like his grandfather Ralph's cars. Dale Jr. won three races, including The Winston, in his rookie season with his uncle Tony Eury Sr. as the crew chief, cousin Tony

Eury Jr. as the car chief and uncle Danny Earnhardt as a tire carrier. When Kerry was fired from a ride in the Busch Series, Earnhardt stepped in there, too, providing his first son with cars to compete in the ARCA series. At the Michigan Speedway in June of 2001, driving under sponsorship from the Kannapolis Intimidators baseball team owned in part by DEI, Kerry became the first Earnhardt to win a race after his father's death.

Racing ultimately held the Earnhardt family together. Dale and Dale Jr. co-drove a Corvette C5-R and finished second in the 24-hour race at Daytona just two weeks before his father's fatal crash. *"This has helped our relationship,"* said Dale Jr. *"Me and him didn't spend that much time together. This was another step toward doing that."*

To the roaring approval of 160,000 fans, in July of 2001 Dale Jr. won the first Winston Cup race at Daytona after the tragic 500, passing Johnny Benson Jr. for the lead in the outside groove in Turn 4, where his father's crash had taken place.

"This has helped our relationship," said Dale Jr. "Me and him didn't spend that much time together. This was another step toward doing that"

PREVIOUS PAGES: The best time to spend time with Dad was at the track. Dale Earnhardt Jr. went short track racing with his father and later daughter Taylor visited victory lane.

LEFT: The Dale Earnhardt Inc. team reflected its resolve by bringing a stout Chevy Monte Carlo to Daytona for Dale Earnhardt Jr. in the first race at the Florida track after the Daytona 500.

TOP RIGHT: Earnhardt Jr. celebrates a courageous win at Daytona, where he made the winning pass in the same turn that claimed his father's life less than five months earlier.

BOTTOM RIGHT: Father and son share an umbrella waiting out a rain delay at Darlington, S.C. during the 2000 season.

ABOVE: At long last, Dale Earnhardt celebrates his first Daytona 500 victory after 19 years of futiliy and near misses at NASCAR's crown jewel.

PAGE 22
TOP: Early in the fateful Daytona 500, Earnhardt hotly contested the lead with everyone, including his son's No.8 Chevy, before a broken air dam forced him to play spoiler for his two DEI entries.

BOTTOM The paint schemes sometimes changed, but the No.3 was ubiquitous. Car owner Richard Childress originally adopted the 3 during his own driving career, a number his wife groused at the time, "would never amount to anything."

PAGE 23
Joe Whitlock, a longtime family friend and PR man at the outset of Earnhardt's Wrangler Jeans sponsorship, called him "the last cowboy."

PAGE 24
TOP: Earnhardt's ninth victory at Talladega in October 1999 was not his greatest. This came the following year when he moved from 21st to first in the closing laps with his patented risky maneuvers.

BOTTOM: The Richard Childress Racing Team celebrates in victory lane at Talladega after Earnhardt's ninth of ten vicories at the 2.66-mile Alabama track.

"I'm Always In A Hurry"

If a driver in the Winston Cup garage suddenly felt a painful pinch on his neck from an unseen adversary, he knew Dale Earnhardt was near. *"That's how he greeted you,"* said Jeff Gordon.

If a driver got a fender popped at high speed, his car briefly unsettled and his emotions likewise skewed, that also was a sign Earnhardt was near. After one such episode coming off Turn 4 at Darlington during Earnhardt's second title season, Richard Petty spun and crashed. *"I forgot I was around Earnhardt,"* said the man known as *"The King."*

Whether in the garage or on the track,

Earnhardt pushed others to the brink just like he pushed himself. *"I'm always in a hurry,"* he said.

Earnhardt's fender-banging wasn't always about gaining a position. At the Atlanta Motor Speedway in 1993, Earnhardt pulled his Chevy alongside the Ford of Alan Kulwicki, the defending Winston Cup champion, and twice popped his opponent's doors. That was Earnhardt's way of telling him *"The Intimidator"* was still the man to beat. *"He just drove right into the side of me,"* said an exasperated Kulwicki of the 175-mph greeting.

Such moments reflected Earnhardt's

rough-and-tumble hometown of Kannapolis, N.C., where some folks would just as soon punch you as shake your hand. But most of Earnhardt's aggression on the track reflected the family's racing creed.

Just as father Ralph Earnhardt would position his short track dirt car versus competitors so they fought for control, spun or let him by, Earnhardt used aerodynamics on the superspeedways to position his car

for the same effect. If bumping ensued at high speed, you either had the skill to prevent a crash—or not. *"If you can't stand the heat,"* Earnhardt would say, *"get out of the kitchen."*

The Winston Cup's biggest, richest races on the high-banked tracks at Daytona and Talladega played to his strong suit. He decried the carburetor restrictors used to keep average lap speeds below 200 mph,

ABOVE: The worst of two major crashes at Talladega came in 1996. After flipping over, Earnhardt's Chevy was hit twice again.

PREVIOUS PAGE: The open-faced helmet gave Earnhardt a wider field of vision, and it enabled competitors to see "The Intimidator" as well.

RIGHT: Earnhardt liked Jeff Gordon, driver of the No. 24 Chevy, because the young star was just as aggressive as he was.

calling drivers who endorsed them *"candy asses."* But the plates put an emphasis on aerodynamic drafting and close quarter racing, which favored Earnhardt. He had more victories at those two tracks than any other driver.

It was said he could see the air, despite sitting low in his car wearing an old-fashioned, open-faced helmet with his head cocked to the left. Earnhardt no doubt had extraordinary powers when it came to the eyesight of his gunmetal blue eyes. *"He would call in on the radio and tell me where a stray bolt was sitting on the track,"* said

Andy Petree, crew chief for his Winston Cup titles in 1993–94.

At six feet and 185 pounds, Earnhardt had shoulders big enough to accept he was in more crashes and controversies due to his own rambunctious style.

He held his greatest affection for those who took his methods in their stride and pushed back, such as Gordon. En route to his first Daytona 500 victory, Gordon put Earnhardt's Chevy on its roof in Turn 2. *"Was I scared?"* said Earnhardt, who would come back to win the race the following year. *"I've never been scared in a race car."*

DEI and the "Garage Mahal"

Very few drivers in NASCAR history turned a steering wheel as well as Dale Earnhardt. But no one came close when it came to turning a profit. After forming Dale Earnhardt Inc. with his wife Teresa, the seven-time champion built a multi-million dollar empire.

On the heels of seven Winston Cup championships, he and Teresa owned an ocean-going yacht called *"Sunday Money,"* a Chevrolet dealership, four airplanes and a Lear Jet, a 350-acre farm with 40,000 chickens, three Winston Cup teams, a share of a minor league baseball team and a seat on the New York Stock Exchange.

The majority of DEI's wealth resulted not from the driver's portion of the $42 million in race purses he won, rather from selling his image on souvenirs, estimated to generate $50 million in sales per year.

Earnhardt described his marriage to Teresa as the best business deal he ever made, and later his business manager, Don Hawk, described her as a *"marketing genius. They were probably the best one-two punch*

in sports." Not long after their marriage, it was Teresa who insisted on forming Dale Earnhardt Inc. in order to take control of the driver's image and trademarks.

They first set up in the barn that had been converted into a garage by Ralph Earnhardt behind the family's house in Kannapolis, N.C., but ended up with offices in what became known as the *"Garage Mahal,"* DEI's swank headquarters in Mooresville, N.C..

It wasn't Earnhardt who established the souvenir market. That honor belonged to seven-time champion Richard Petty, who helped finance his retirement with collectibles sold on his Fan Appreciation Tour in 1992. But once the market began to expand dramatically with Petty's tour and the burgeoning popularity of NASCAR, the Earnhardts were in the best position to exploit it.

For nine years, their souvenir business was handled by Sports Image Inc., which paid DEI a royalty for use of the driver's image. The Earnhardts then bought the company from Hank Jones and a partner for an estimated $6 million in 1995, a move

ABOVE: Dale Earnhardt Inc. joined the Winston Cup in 1998 with one entry driven by Steve Park (left). A Chevy for Dale Earnhardt Jr. (center) was added in 2000 before DEI became a three-car team with Michael Waltrip (right) in 2001.

"pushing the level of our business through the roof"

that drew high praise. *"It's a very smart move,"* said one sports marketing executive. *"He can carefully craft the image he puts out there."* Earnhardt *"is pushing the level of our business through the roof,"* said driver Kyle Petty, also the CEO of Petty Enterprises and a leader in souvenir sales. *"He harnessed everything together in a way that no one has really thought of before."*

The company's major product remained the image of the *"Intimidator."* In exchange for royalties, the company also had the rights to the image of the team where he

drove, Richard Childress Racing, the image of the team's GM Goodwrench sponsor, and had deals with General Motors, the manufacturer of Chevy. It all resulted from Earnhardt's hard bargaining.

The acquisition of Sports Image was just the beginning. Within two years, Sports Image was sold to Action Performance, a collectibles company, for $30 million. And, DEI retained control of all images of the *"Intimidator."*

Not bad for a kid from Kannapolis who never made it past the ninth grade.

Beating the All-Stars

The made-for-TV races that evolved in the 1970s and 1980s were made to order for Dale Earnhardt, because these shorter events emphasized individual skill and aggressiveness. Earnhardt won six of NASCAR's 50-mile *"shootout"* exhibitions, the season-opening ice-breakers at Daytona. In 1993, Earnhardt became the first three-time winner of The Winston, NASCAR's All-Star race. And he won the International Race of Champions title four times.

"The Intimidator" used his persona for maximum benefit in these races, where caution could be jettisoned since drivers were competing for money and prestige, but not the precious points needed for a Winston Cup.

In 1987, at the Charlotte track where his father Ralph used to bring him to watch races from the back of a pick-up truck, Earnhardt caused a major uproar in The Winston with a move that became known, however erroneously, as *"The Pass In The Grass."*

In the final ten-lap dash for $200,000, Earnhardt had taken the lead from fourth place by bumping leader Bill Elliott at the start. When the significantly faster *"Awesome Bill"* tried to retake the lead moving underneath at the track's dogleg, Earnhardt pulled down to block him and caught his rear bumper on the nose of Elliott's Ford. That sent Earnhardt's Chevy sideways into the grass, where he made a miraculous recovery and returned to the track without losing the lead. He later rode Elliott into the Turn 3 wall in anger, moving the Georgia redhead to retaliate by hitting Earnhardt's Chevy on the cool down lap.

The race set off a heated debate about Earnhardt's tactics that would continue for the remainder of his career. *"That's the style he's comfortable with," said retired two-time champion Ned Jarrett. *"He likes to get in there, root around and run close, just like his father did."*

In 1993, under the lighting system installed the previous year, Earnhardt used pure psychology to win The Winston. From the outside front row, he deliberately jumped the final re-start with two laps to go against the dominating Ford of Mark Martin. Fearing he had lost the race after Earnhardt sped away, when NASCAR called for another start and re-grouped the field for a second green flag a deflated Martin gave up the lead again, this time in Turn 3. Earnhardt led only the last two laps to win.

No less gentle with his fenders in the IROC series, Earnhardt tagged the rear of Al Unser Jr.'s Dodge at Turn 3 on the last lap to win at Daytona in 1995, moving some observers from open-wheel racing to call his tactics primitive.

But Earnhardt used cerebral methods as well. In 1991, Englishman Martin Brundle was leading the IROC points coming into the final race at the 2.0-mile Michigan oval. Brundle's wife was close to delivering a child at the time. *"I'll never forget the first five words Dale Earnhardt said to me,"* recalled the Le Mans 24-hour winner with a smile. *"Just before the start at Michigan, he walked past my car and said, 'Remember the wife and kid.'"* Brundle crashed after spinning and "The Intimidator" won his second IROC title.

LEFT: Earnhardt used a variety of paint schemes as well as tactics in The Winston under the lights at Charlotte Motor Speedway.

ABOVE: Nine of Earnhardt's 11 victories in IROC came at his favorite tracks of Talladega and Daytona. The other two were scored at Michigan. He's shown here with the trophy from Talladega in 1999.

The Last Daytona 500

Dale Earnhardt walked tall everywhere on the Winston Cup circuit, but he was the boss at Daytona. Having won the crown jewel Daytona 500 in 1998, he arrived at Speed Weeks in 2001 with a record 34 victories on the storied high banks of NASCAR's most famous track.

NASCAR had mandated new roof blades and larger rear spoilers, using aerodynamics to slow cars and create more passing. The driver of the Richard Childress Racing Chevy always chafed at such changes, which reduced the pole speed to 184 mph. *"What's the problem with running 200?"* said Earnhardt.

The new rules as well as the new factory Dodges led by the silver Intrepid of Sterling Marlin created furious maneuvering at the front of the field. On lap 27, Earnhardt's Chevy took the lead from Marlin at Turn 3 and held it for 11 circuits. But on his first pit stop, Earnhardt collided briefly with the Pontiac of Ken Schrader entering the pits, damaging his front air dam.

Undaunted, Earnhardt returned to the

ABOVE: Once the Chevy's of Waltrip (leading), Earnhardt Jr. and Earnhardt formed a line in the lower groove, Marlin had a tough time passing in his solo Dodge.

RIGHT: Moments after colliding with the Turn 4 wall, the Chevy of Earnhardt drifts back down the banking along with the Pontiac of Ken Schrader.

lead on three more occasions. On the 183rd of 200 laps, he sliced between the Chevy of Michael Waltrip and Marlin in the narrow Turn 3 with a stunning attack. But the faulty air damn, which hampered his speed while leading, forced Earnhardt to quickly fall back behind the Dale Earnhardt Inc. entries of Waltrip and Dale Earnhardt Jr.

With ten laps to go, the three Chevy drivers formed a line in the low groove. Earnhardt began a rear guard action to hold third place and help his drivers up ahead in the DEI Monte Carlos.

On lap 196, Earnhardt shut down Marlin's strong bid at the inside of Turn 3 by blocking. Two laps later, Schrader failed in his bid to get around the three Chevys by taking the high groove at Turn 1. On the 199th circuit, eventual winner Waltrip and runner-up Earnhardt Jr. broke away when third-placed Earnhardt blocked Schrader and Marlin again at the tri-oval bend, setting up a fateful final lap.

At the end of the back straight, Schrader made a bid to pass on the high side of Earnhardt again at Turn 3, Marlin took the low route and the Ford of Rusty Wallace pulled up close to the rear of Earnhardt's Chevy. Still fighting the broken air damn, on worn tires now and without any drafting help, the black No. 3 Chevy was surrounded by faster adversaries and turbulent air.

With his car wobbling, Earnhardt's errant left rear hit the nose of the Dodge as Marlin bid to pass at the lower edge of the track midway between Turns 3 and 4. Perhaps caught out by his broken air dam, the new aerodynamics—or both—Earnhardt overcorrected and his Chevy's tail swerved down the track as a result and hooked its left rear tire on the flat apron. As both Marlin and Wallace stormed past, the black Chevy shot up the banking, caroming off Schrader's Pontiac.

Earnhardt died instantly from the head-on impact with the Turn 4 wall.

"Somebody Pinned The Right Name On Him"

NASCAR Chairman Bill France Jr. called Dale Earnhardt *"the greatest driver in the history of the sport"* shortly after his fatal accident. It was the beginning of the struggle by participants and fans with the fact that a living legend was gone.

"A lot of people who weren't involved in Winston Cup racing before Dale Earnhardt got here couldn't imagine what it was like without him," said Steve Hmiel, the technical director for Dale Earnhardt Inc. *"But there's a lot of people who were here before Dale Earnhardt came in and they still felt like he was what the sport was all about. He was just cool."*

"I don't think you can put into words what he meant to the sport," said Jeff Gordon. *"There's no one like him. We're not going to just miss him on the racetrack. We're going to miss his presence in the garage and with the fans."*

RIGHT: "We shared a common bond in championships as well as a mutual respect," said Richard Petty.

That was a sentiment backed up by other drivers. *"He helped so many people in the garage and then he walked over to his car and he was the 'Intimidator,'"* said Jeremy Mayfield.

"If you had an autograph session with the Winston Cup drivers, three times as many people would be lined up for Earnhardt," said Jimmy Spencer. *"Everybody wanted to meet John Wayne."*

Not only was Earnhardt a racing great, but an all-American legend as well. *"I've watched Michael Jordan and Tiger Woods compete and Dale Earnhardt was as intense as either one of them,"* said Don Hawk, his former business manager. *"He was one of the 50 greatest athletes ever. He had a swagger to his walk and he could*

ABOVE: The death of Earnhardt had a far-reaching impact. Here the Chicago White Sox pause for a moment of silence during spring training.

BELOW: "He liked to push people to their limits," said Darrell Waltrip (right). "But all the same, he was the standard bearer for professional drivers."

OVERLEAF: Atlanta Braves Manager Bobby Cox (above) knew Dale well . Richard Childress (below) was a friend, mentor and car owner. "Never giving up. That's what made Dale great," he said.

talk the talk."

Earnhardt developed many friendships outside the racing world in the spheres of business and sports. One of his closest friends, Ned Yost, a coach for the Atlanta Braves baseball club, said there was much more to the private man than his racing image. *"We hunted together for 12 years,"* said Yost. *"He taught me how to be a friend. He taught me how to be a better husband and how to be a better competitor and how to never give up."*

Braves' manager, Bobby Cox, a lifelong racing enthusiast, became friends with Earnhardt through Yost. *"Dale Earnhardt was NASCAR,"* said Cox. *"But he made his mark in the hearts of all racing fans."* Cox, who directed the Braves to victory in the 1995 World Series, then told the story of the day he drove with Earnhardt to a test at the Talladega Superspeedway in Alabama.

"We were going in the back way to the track on a two-lane road," said Cox. *"About a quarter mile down the road, there was a van coming toward us. Earnhardt pulled his car into the oncoming lane and told me, 'You watch. This guy's going to change lanes.' We were headed straight at the van and sure enough, at the last second the guy changes lanes to go around our car.*

"I realized right then why they called this guy the 'Intimidator.' Somebody pinned the right name on him."

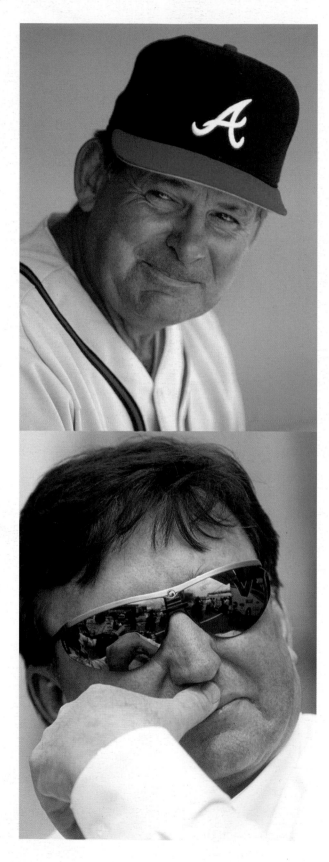

The Aftermath

Not since 1964 and the fiery, fatal crash of Fireball Roberts in Charlotte had there been such an outcry in NASCAR racing. But typical of his career, nothing matched the response to Dale Earnhardt's fatal accident on the last lap of the Daytona 500.

windows of pick-up trucks across the country.

The wailing did not come just from fans. The intense media coverage continued when NASCAR officials announced five days after the accident that a torn lap belt on the safety harness had been discovered, raising questions of just how the driver died and

ABOVE: The rescue effort became controversial when a broken seat belt was not revealed to the media until five days later.

ABOVE: Fans created an impromptu memorial at the entrance to the Garage Mahal, where flags flew at half staff.

In death, Earnhardt remained a major force in the growth of stock car racing, contributing more to the public awareness of it than ever before due to mainstream media coverage. Fans, meanwhile, left a sea of flowers, signs, ribbons, and balloons at the entrance to Dale Earnhardt Inc. Decals of the tilted number 3 outlined in red, just like those on Earnhardt's car, flourished on the back

about the sanctioning body's credibility.

Other questions focused on the fact three drivers had been killed by similar meetings with the wall during the 2000 season at other tracks in NASCAR's Winston Cup, Busch and Craftsman Truck series. But it was not until after Earnhardt's death that the sanctioning body launched a full-scale crash investigation.

The media followed its own pursuit. A

BELOW: Memorials and vigils sprung up across the country, including this one at "The Rock" outside the track in Rockingham, N.C.

BELOW: Mike Helton, president of NASCAR, announces the seven-time champion's death in the media center at Daytona.

high-profile lawsuit resulted from Teresa Earnhardt's legal efforts to block access to her husband's autopsy photos by the *Orlando Sentinel* newspaper, due to concerns about such photos being used by less scrupulous outlets posting them on Internet web sites. Eventually, a new law was passed by the Florida legislature after lobbying by the late driver's wife that required a judge's consent to autopsy photo access.

Prior to that, an agreement was reached between Teresa Earnhardt and the *Sentinel*'s lawyers, and a medical expert viewed the autopsy photos. Dr. Barry Myers concluded in his report to the *Sentinel* that head whip—when the helmet and head were catapulted forward upon impact—led to a fatal fracture at the base of the skull. Another crash expert, John Melvin, said that the torn belt was not likely a factor and resulted from the same

loading that caused the fatal head injury.

The message was clear. Where four drivers wore head restraints in the Daytona 500, five months later 33 of the 43 starters wore head restraints in the Pepsi 400 at Daytona.

Earnhardt had no interest in a head restraint, which required a full-face helmet instead of his preferred open-face style. Vitally interested in safety such as the development of soft walls instead, Earnhardt still thought racing should be the home of the brave. At Daytona prior to the July race in 2000, the driver said as much to his fellow competitors, calling some of them chicken. *"Don't come here and grumble about going too fast,"* he said in the midst of the safety debate that erupted due to the death of Adam Petty, the first driver killed that year. *"Stay the hell home. Get out of the car if you've got feathers on your backside."*

Statistics

NASCAR Winston Cup Championship Seasons

Year	Races	Car	Car Owner	Crew Chief	Wins	Top Five	Top 10	Poles	Winnings
1980	31	Chevy Monte Carlo	Rod Osterlund	Jake Elder & Doug Richert	5	19	23	0	$588,926
1986	29	Chevy Monte Carlo	Richard Childress	Kirk Shelmerdine	5	16	23	1	$1,783,880
1987	29	Chevy Monte Carlo	Richard Childress	Kirk Shelmerdine	11	21	24	1	$2,099,243
1990	29	Chevy Lumina	Richard Childress	Kirk Shelmerdine	9	18	23	4	$3,083,056
1991	29	Chevy Lumina	Richard Childress	Kirk Shelmderdine	4	14	21	0	$2,396,685
1993	30	Chevy Lumina	Richard Childress	Andy Petree	6	17	21	2	$3,353,789
1994	31	Chevy Lumina	Richard Childress	Andy Petree	4	20	25	2	$3,300,733

NASCAR Winston Cup Wins

	Date	Track	Miles	Winnings

1979 Car owner: Rod Osterlund, Car: Chevy Monte Carlo, Crew Chief: Jake Elder

	Date	Track	Miles	Winnings
1.	April 1	Bristol Int. Raceway	266.5	$19,800

1980 Crew Chief(s): Jake Elder, *Doug Richert

	Date	Track	Miles	Winnings
2.	Mar 16	Atlanta International Raceway	500	$36,200
3.	Mar 30	Bristol Int. Raceway	266.5	$20,625
4.	July 12	Nashville Int. Raceway*	250	$14,600
5.	Sept 28	Martinsville Speedway*	263	$25,375
6.	Oct 5	Charlotte Motor Speedway*	500	$49,050

1982 Car owner: Bud Moore, Car: Ford Thunderbird, Crew Chief: Bud Moore

	Date	Track	Miles	Winnings
7.	April 4	Darlington Raceway	500	$31,450

1983

	Date	Track	Miles	Winnings
8.	July 16	Nashville Int. Raceway	250	$23,125
9.	July 31	Alabama Int. Motor Speedway	500	$46,950

1984 Car owner: Richard Childress, Car: Chevy Monte Carlo, Crew Chief: Kirk Shelmerdine

	Date	Track	Miles	Winnings
10.	July 29	Alabama Int. Motor Speedway	500	$47,100
11.	Nov 11	Atlanta Int. Raceway	500	$40,610

1985

	Date	Track	Miles	Winnings
12.	Feb. 24	Richmond Fairgrounds Raceway	216.8	$33,625
13.	April 6	Bristol Int. Raceway	266.5	$31,525
14.	Aug 24	Bristol Int. Raceway	266.5	$34,675
15.	Sept 22	Martinsville Speedway	263	$37,725

1986

	Date	Track	Miles	Winnings
16.	April 13	Darlington Raceway	500	$52,250
17.	April 20	North Wilkesboro Speedway	250	$38,550
18.	May 25	Charlotte Motor Speedway	600	$98,150
19.	Oct 5	Charlotte Motor Speedway	500	$82,050
20.	Nov. 2	Atlanta Int. Raceway	500	$67,950

1987

	Date	Track	Miles	Winnings
21.	Mar 1	N.C. Motor Speedway	500	$53,9002
22.	Mar 8	Richmond Fairgrounds Raceway	216.8	$49,150
23.	Mar 29	Darlington Raceway	500	$52,985
24.	April 5	North Wilkesboro Speedway	260	$44,677
25.	April 12	Bristol Int. Raceway	266.5	$43,850
26.	April 26	Martinsville Speedway	263	$50,850
27.	June 28	Michigan Int. Speedway	400	$60,250
28.	July 19	Pocono Int. Raceway	500	$55,875
29.	Aug 22	Bristol Int. Raceway	266.5	$47,175
30.	Sept 6	Darlington Raceway	276	$64,650
31.	Sept 13	Richmond Fairgrounds Raceway	216.8	$44,950

1988

	Date	Track	Miles	Winnings
32.	Mar 20	Atlanta Int. Raceway	500	$67,950
33.	April 24	Martinsville Speedway	263	$53,550
34.	Aug 27	Bristol Int. Raceway	266.5	$48,500

1989 Car: Chevy Lumina

	Date	Track	Miles	Winnings
35.	April 16	North Wilkesboro Speedway*	260	$51,225
36.	June 4	Dover Downs Int. Speedway	500	$59,350
37.	Sept 3	Darlington Raceway	500	$71,150
38.	Sept 17	Dover Downs Int. Speedway	500	$59,950
39.	Nov 19	Atlanta Int. Raceway	500	$81,700

*Chevy Monte Carlo

1990

	Date	Track	Miles	Winnings
40.	Mar 18	Atlanta Int. Raceway	500	$85,000
41.	April 1	Darlington Raceway	500	$61,985
42.	May 6	*Talladega Superspeedway	500	$98,975
43.	June 24	Michigan Int. Speedway	400	$72,950
44.	July 7	Daytona Int. Speedway	400	$72,850
45.	July 29	*Talladega Superspeedway	500	$152,975
46.	Sept	Darlington Raceway	500	$110,350
47.	Sept 9	**Richmond Int. Raceway	300	$59,225
48.	Nov 4	Phoenix Int Raceway	312	$72,100

*Formerly Alabama Int. Motor Speedway

**Formerly Richmond Fairgrounds Raceway

	Date	Track	Miles	Winnings
1991				
49	Feb 24	Richmond Int. Raceway	300	$67,950
50	April 28	Martinsville Speedway	263	$63,600
51	July 28	Talladega Superspeedway	500	$88,670
52	Sept. 29	North Wilkesboro Speedway	260	$69,350
1992				
53	May 24	Charlotte Motor Speedway	600	$125,100
1993 *Crew chief: Andy Petree*				
54	Mar. 28	Darlington Raceway	500	$64,815
55	May 30	Charlotte Motor Speedway	600	$156,650
56	June 6	Dover Downs Int. Speedway	500	$68,030
57	July 3	Daytona Int. Speedway	400	$75,940
58	July 18	Pocono Int. Raceway	500	$66,795
59	July 25	Talladega Superspeedway	500	$87,315
1994				
60.	Mar. 27	Darlington Raceway	257	$70,190
61.	April 10	*Bristol Motor Speedway	266.5	$72,570
62.	May 1	Talladega Superspeedway	500	$94,865
63.	Oct 23	N.C. Motor Speedway	500	$60,600

Formerly Bristol Int. Raceway

	Date	Track	Miles	Winnings
1995 *Car: Chevy Monte Carlo*				
64.	April 9	North Wilkesboro Speedway	260	$77,400
65.	May 7	Sears Point Raceway	197	$74,860
66.	Aug 5	Indianapolis Motor Speedway	400	$565,600
67.	Sept 24	Martinsville Speedway	263	$78,150
68.	Nov 12	*Atlanta Motor Speedway	500	$141,850

Formerly Atlanta Int. Raceway

	Date	Track	Miles	Winnings
1996 *Crew Chief: David Smith*				
69.	Feb. 25	N.C. Motor Speedway	400	$83,840
70.	Mar. 10	Atlanta Motor Speedway	500	$91,050
1998 *Crew Chief: Larry McReynolds*				
71.	Feb. 15	Daytona Int. Speedway	500	$1,059,805
1999 *Crew Chief: Kevin Hamlin*				
72.	April 25	Talladega Superspeedway	500	$147,795
73.	Aug. 28	Bristol Motor Speedway	266.5	$89,880
74.	Oct. 17	Talladega Superspeedway	500	$120,290
2000				
75.	Mar. 12	Atlanta Motor Speedway	500	$123,100
76.	Oct. 15	Talladega Superspeedway	500	$135,900

TOTALS:
Starts: 676
Wins: 76 (48 on superspeedways)
Poles: 22 (17 on superspeedways)
Front row starts: 52
Top Five: 281
Top 10: 428
Money won: $41,708,384

Winston Cup Poles:

Atlanta Motor Speedway
1982, 1986, 1987, 1995

Bristol Motor Speedway
1985, 1990

Darlington Raceway
1990

Daytona Int. Speedway
1994, 1995, 1996

Dover Downs Int. Speedway
1979

North Wilkesboro Speedway
1979

Richmond Int. Raceway
1979, 1995

Riverside Int. Raceway
1979

Sears Point Raceway
1993

Talladega Superspeedway
1990, 1993, 1994

Watkins Glen International
1990, 1992, 1996

Twin 125-mile Qualifying Race Victories At Daytona (12)
1983, 1986, 1990, 1991, 1992, 1993,
1994, 1995, 1996, 1997, 1998, 1999

International Race of Champions
Championships: **1990, 1995, 1999, 2000**

Victories:
IROC XIV (1990)
May 5, Talladega Superspeedway
Aug. 5, Michigan Int. Speedway

IROC XVI (1992)
Feb. 14, Daytona Int. Speedway
IROC XVIII (1994)
Feb. 18, Daytona Int. Speedway

IROC XIX (1995)
Feb. 17, Daytona Int. Speedway
April 29, Talladega Superspeedway

IROC XX (1996)
Feb. 16, Daytona Int. Speedway

IROC XXIII (1999)
Feb. 12, Daytona Int. Speedway
April 24, Talladega Superspeedway
June 11, Michigan Int. Speedway

IROC XXIV (2000)
Feb. 18, Daytona Int. Speedway

Busch Series Victories

Track	Miles	Car	Car owner
1982			
Daytona Int. Speedway	300	Pontiac	Robert Gee
Caraway Speedway	100	Olds	Ed Whitaker
1983			
N.C. Motor Speedway	200	Pontiac	Robert Gee
Charlotte Motor Speedway	300	Pontiac	Robert Gee
1985			
N.C. Motor Speedway	200	Pontiac	Teresa Earnhardt
1986			
Daytona Int. Speedway	300	Pontiac	Teresa Earnhardt
N.C. Motor Speedway	200	Pontiac	Teresa Earnhardt
Darlington Raceway	200	Pontiac	Teresa Earnhardt
Richmond Fairgrounds Raceway	108	Chevy	Teresa Earnhardt
Charlotte Motor Speedway	300	Pontiac	Teresa Earnhardt
1987			
Darlington Raceway	200	Chevy	Teresa Earnhardt
1988			
Bristol Int. Raceway	106	Chevy	Teresa Earnhardt

Track	Miles	Car	Car owner
1990			
Daytona Int. Speedway	300	Chevy	Teresa Earnhardt
N.C. Motor Speedway	200	Chevy	Teresa Earnhardt
1991			
Daytona Int. Speedway	300	Chevy	Teresa Earnhardt
Charlotte Motor Speedway	300	Chevy	Teresa Earnhardt
Darlington Raceway	200	Chevy	Teresa Earnhardt
1992			
Daytona Int. Speedway	300	Chevy	Teresa Earnhardt
1993			
Daytona Int. Speedway	300	Chevy	Teresa Earnhardt
Talladega Superspeedway	312	Chevy	Teresa Earnhardt
1994			
Daytona Int. Speedway	300	Chevy	Teresa Earnhardt

TOTALS: Wins: 21 (18 superspeedway)
Poles: 7

Dale Earnhardt Inc. Championship Seasons

Year	Driver	Wins	Top Five	Top 10	Poles	Entry	Winnings
NASCAR Busch Series							
1998	Dale Earnhardt Jr.	7	16	22	3	Chevy	$1,332,701
1999	Dale Earnhardt Jr.	6	18	22	5	Chevy	$1,680,599
NASCAR Craftsman Truck Series							
1996	Ron Hornaday	4	18	23	2	Chevy	$625,634
1998	Ron Hornaday	6	16	22	2	Chevy	$915,407

ABOUT THE AUTHOR

JONATHAN INGRAM has written about the world's major motor racing series for the past 25 years. In addition to premium web sites, the Atlanta-based writer's work has appeared in over 100 magazines and newspapers on four continents. He first met Dale Earnhardt during the driver's rookie year in the Winston Cup in 1979 and considers one of the highlights of his career a dinner with Earnhardt and his wife Teresa in London during the Autosport Awards banquet in 1996.

The publishers would like to thank the following sources for their kind permission to reproduce the pictures in this book:

Allsport USA: p.5t, 5b, 5l, 20, 21t, 21b, 22t, 22b, 23, 27, 28r, 29, 32, 36, 39t, 40b, 40t, 42l, 43r, 43l, 45, 47

Corbis: p.28l, 42r

Sutton Motorsport Images: p.3, 4, 19, 24b, 25, 26, 31, 33, 34-35, 38, 39b

Popperfoto: p.37

International Motor Sports Hall of Fame: p.6-7, 8tl, 8tr, 8b, 9, 11, 12-13, 15, 18

Every effort has been made to acknowledge correctly and contact the source and/copyright holder of each picture, and Carlton Books apologises for any unintentional errors or omissions which will be corrected in future editions of this book.